Ketchup for Your Sales Process!

----- "A Guide to Sales Success!"

Written for you, the Sales Manager as well as the Sales Rep in the field.

Copyright @ 2018 3LConsulting Group

Cover Design: Roger Ciliberto

3LConsulting Group
ISBN-13: 978-0578208039
ISBN-10: 0578208032
BISAC: Business & Economics / Skills

Roger Ciliberto
3LConsulting Group
Hilton NY 14468 – 781-330-8480

Ketchup for Your Sales Process!

Special Thanks to Jaret Christopher who got me my start on a trigger based sales approach, as well as the friendships of James Cabral and Matt Conway for their encouragement and motivation throughout the years....

Forward

Everyone loves a good cheeseburger. And when you are really hungry a cheeseburger on its own can be really good. But I think it's the ketchup that makes it even better!

There are many sales people who are doing some really good selling. Over the last 20-years, I have led several sales teams and have come up with different techniques and processes that have worked more often than not. I have learned from many great minds and have been fortunate enough to have been exposed to many different software offerings and solutions… several from their infancy, (…. I remember the early days of salesforce.com). I am hoping some of these experiences can be your "Ketchup". Making your selling, …. *even better!*

Within the following chapters are my experiences, as well as how you as a sales person or a leader can become better at your craft by following some simple steps and utilizing some simple programs that make life a bit easier in the professional selling world.

My goal was to summarize all that I have come across over these years and give you the opportunity to tap into my success and maybe make some of it your own. I will also discuss some of the different sales software that is available to you. There are new offerings coming out seemingly every day. With the onslaught of Artificial Intelligence and Machine Learning, companies like *DataHug, Conversica, LeadSpace* and countless others, can potentially help you accomplish much of what I am soon to outline in the chapters ahead.

Many of these solutions offer trials that you should take advantage of and see which will work best for you and your organization.

About Me:

I have spent almost 20-years leading sales team's selling SaaS. Originally from Upstate NY, I began my career at 3M company and have held many roles building and leading teams in both New York and the Boston MA market.

In Boston, I worked for a startup called TrueAdvantage which delivered a SaaS lead gen software to companies in need of sales leads. After two successful years, I was asked to open a remote branch in Rochester, NY where my team outsold the corporate location almost twofold.

After TrueAdvantage endured a series of setbacks, new ownership relocated me back to Massachusetts in 2005 to set up an Inside Sales team at the new Corporate HQ in Southborough, MA. I was then appointed VP of Sales.

After the VC's appointed our third CEO in just a few months, I decided to test the waters and in January 2008, I joined Reed Business Interactive ('RBI'), a subsidiary of Reed Elsevier.

At Reed, I was hired to build an inside sales team focusing on securing online ads for this publishing and marketing firm. I built a team of ten reps. The inside team grew to 18 by mid-2009 and continued its success. Reed eventually announced the pending sale of RBI in 2009 and eventually began to sell off parts of my organization which led me to seek new opportunities.

At Avention/OneSource (Now D&B/Hoovers), I continued to lead a new business sales organization in selling SaaS which leverages Sales 2.0 and partnerships. My team, increased revenue quarter over quarter as Avention continued to release new products and cutting edge solutions to help sales organizations achieve quotas.

After a brief stay at NetBrain where I built an enterprise sales team of 10, in 2016, I launched the new US sales team for Companybook.   Today, I am President of 3LConsulting Group helping organizations set up the processes needed to make their sales teams successful. Visit us at www.rogerciliberto.com to learn more.

Contents:

Chapter 1

As a Sales Rep, How Do You

Determine 'Who's Buying'?

"Do I believe in my heart of hearts that what I am selling can help the prospect and people I will potentially speak to, to satisfy their NEED"?

On average, each day, I receive roughly ten to fifteen, emails and Linked-In outreaches trying to sell me recruiting, lead-generation, appointment setting, marketing help and some others. Although I appreciate the effort, its usually 11:00 AM by the time I receive my 10th outreach!!! And although I run a sales team and have <u>my reps doing the same exact thing</u>, at the end of the day there is simply ONE thing that will lead my team or even you to a prospect or a "real" lead where there is explicit interest in what you are selling.... What is that ONE thing? ....Its *NEED*.

Simply put, does the prospect you are reaching out to have a NEED for what you are offering?

How many guru's out there will tell you that, THIS is how to write an email and THIS is how to form a subject line and THIS is when you need to send a mail blast, and blah, blah, blah, blah.... Everyone has the answers to more connects. They say to, "Sound confident", "do the research", "have a process".... *No Kidding!*

The reality of sales is even simpler than all the chatter.... Studies show that most buyers are already doing the research. They are 60+% through the buying process without even speaking to a rep. The trick is to uncover the needle in the haystack. Where are these people and how do I find them? These are the guru's we need to listen to.

Before we decide on how we find them... You need to ask yourself this: "Do I believe in my heart of hearts that what I am selling can help the prospect and people I will potentially speak to, to satisfy their NEED"? If the answer is yes, then you have the CONFIDENCE you'll need to pique someone's interest when the need is uncovered. If not, get your resume ready....

Second: Do you have the knowledge you need that will relay the value you offer to your prospect, once isolated? I read an article that says the human attention span is 8-seconds. Can you grab someone's attention in 8-seconds? That sounds impossible. But break it down. If you can grab someone's attention in 8 seconds, more than likely you will get another 20 or so to get them to believe you. If your pitch isn't compelling and you lack the confidence/knowledge and your belief in your solution isn't strong enough.... GAME OVER! You lose. Sound knowledgeable. Sound original. Sound credible. Be likable. These will all assist you on getting to the next step in the process.

But how about that NEED? I have said before even with a need uncovered, you and the personality you bring to the table will play a large part in winning the deal. If a prospect likes you, more so than the competition...then in the event of a tie.... YOU WIN! So hone those personality skills and try and make a connection. Don't fake it. Be genuine. This will help you win more than you lose.

It is true that a process will also help you win more than you lose. Without a process, you will miss steps, miss calls, miss outreaches. So whether its Miller Heiman, Sandler, Top-Down, Bottom-Up, etc. have a process and follow it religiously. They all have their merit, but only if you use it within a system and within a process. Don't be part-time. Follow the process regardless of what it is.

OK, OK, OK.... but the NEED! How do I find the NEED?!

There is no secret in uncovering a NEED. The process helps you work your way to a decision maker and work your way through the buying cycle, but uncovering the NEED so you can utilize your process can be as easy as following these TWO simple steps:

1. **Subscribe to a service that alerts** you to funding announcements, management changes, relocation, hiring and more (Avention/OneSource, recently renamed D&B Hoovers, Google Alerts, RainKing Scoops to name a few). Some examples: If a company has received VC to expand their footprint globally, then that

means they have a NEED for people, real estate, technology, translation services, etc... If a company is building a data center, they have a NEED for racks, IT services, people, equipment and more. Use these triggers to uncover the NEED and leverage this need into using your best 8-second pitch to get someone to listen to your next 20-seconds!

2. **Linked-In Group and community chat boards** are a haven for uncovering NEED. Join as many as you can that are pertinent to the business that you are in. Make it a priority to read and learn what the NEEDS are of those in the group. DON'T SELL ANYTHING IN THESE GROUPS, but rather make suggestions to those who make comments like, *"Our HRIS software sucks, anyone using a service they like?"* I think we may have uncovered a NEED. Whatever groups you join, you will see many people asking for help from everything from IT management software, to technical questions, to suggestions on different vendors to pursue.

At the risk of sounding like a guru, these are simply just a couple

suggestions that have worked for me through the years as a

sales leader. Two very simple ways to uncover the NEED that

we all look for. So spend less time crafting that email or writing

that perfect subject line, or wondering when to send that

blast... you will have time for that later. Find the NEED and

uncover the opportunity which will help you grow your sales

numbers to the dizzying heights you deserve!

Chapter 2

Metrics, Success and You!

"...what you do at anything is what you do at everything".

In this chapter, I would like to focus on process and breaking away from the norm. If you work or lead a sales team, specifically an inside sales team, you know how much focus is put on metrics as they relate to your success. Whether its calls made, talk-time, demo's scheduled, etc. etc. These are the lead indicators that say if you do them in volume, more likely than not your team will be successful.

I think most reps WANT to be successful, and know for the most part what they need to do to be successful. But they lack the discipline and the leadership to achieve in some cases. There is absolutely some truth that the metrics above can lead to success, but reps should ask themselves two questions; first, am I comfortable doing something that makes me successful? And, am I doing it because the metrics say I will be successful if I do it?

Stepping out of the comfort zone and doing the things that YOU KNOW will make you successful is the first step. A study done not too long ago by *Outreach,* speaks to the amount of touches needed to get a reply from a prospect. It states that your best chance to make a connection with a prospect is at the 5th touch and then drops off after that.

1st Touch - 5% connect

2nd Touch - 12% connect

3rd Touch - 18% connect

4th Touch - 21% connect

5th Touch - 28% connect

6th Touch - 10% connect

So with this knowledge, you would think EVERY sales rep would have a consistent process of utilizing their CRM and ensuring that follow up tasks are entered and consistent follow up is completed to get to this 5th touch and stack the deck in their favor. Yet, if you look into any CRM across any inside sales team, you will see leads touched once or twice, then orphaned. Also, how many sales leaders are tracking this metric as a means to tracking success?

Another metric that I have spoken of at length is utilizing an event like a management change or new office opening, or another event to open a door for your sales rep at a time when the odds are a purchase is more likely to be made. *DiscoverOrg* states that 80% of new CTO's named to a new enterprise will make $1M dollars in buying decisions in the first 90-days. *Craig Elias* of *ShiFT Selling* says that a management change leads to a sale 10x's more often. A *Forrester* study shows that when a seller contacts a company who is in buy mode (based on an event occurring at their location), rather than the buyer reaching out to the seller, that they win the business 74% of the time.

These metrics again show that if a process is followed, and followed consistently, that success can be had more often than not based on the numbers and studies completed.

Earlier I said that the two questions a rep needs to ask themselves are; if they are comfortable doing the things that they know will make them successful AND am I doing these things because the metrics say that I will be successful if I do it. If you break up your strategy into two categories; Performance and Results, start to define them like this:

- **Performance**: The things you need to do to get the results you want
- **Results**: A byproduct of performance

Knowing what you need to do to be successful now is defined as the discipline you need to exhibit to do the things that will work AND consistently. Break out of your comfort zone and start doing the things that WILL make you successful.

I watched a video the other day where *Simon Sinek* said, "what you do at anything, is what you do at everything". This hit home for me and it should for you as well. Being successful and doing the things you know you need to do to be successful is breaking from the comfort zone. Following the metrics that WILL make you successful. I believe, that this will not only help you in your work life, but it will help you in all walks of life.

The only way to know if this is true, is to start doing these things TODAY! Don't wait.

Leverage the tools that are available that get you the data you need to stack the deck in your favor. Whether that be CRM, a Data Provider, or whatever. Start doing the things you need to do and start experiencing the success you deserve.

Chapter 3

Is Hoping Your Sale Will Close,

Enough?

What is the most important thing in sales?

It was once said that, ".... Belief (hope) is not a sales strategy." But yet every day in a forecast review a sales rep will utter the words, "I hope it will close this month."

So how do we transfer "hope" or "belief" into concrete sales bookings? That is the million-dollar question. There are so many guru's and processes professing that their strategy or way is the best way to close a sale; SPIN Selling, Solution Selling, Top Down Selling, Bottom-Up Selling, Strategic Selling, Challenger, Miller Heiman, Sandler, it goes on and on...

They all are right in their own way and each process can lead to sales. But there are two key elements to winning a deal no matter who you are using or which way you are being asked to sell:

1. The belief in your heart of hearts that the product you are selling can and will help your prospect achieve the goals you are promising.

2. A process (no matter what it is), that is followed consistently and refined after each misstep to ensure success every step along the way.

Without hope and without belief how compelling can you be? Without structure and without a process can you be consistent in closing a sale?

If as a sales rep, you have no faith in your product, 9 times out of 10 that will be felt by those you are selling to. Conversely, if you have a passion for your solution and you KNOW it will lead to your prospects success, that as well will be felt by the decision makers you are selling to. Which one do you think leads to more success? If you don't believe in the products or services you are selling, it's time to move on and find something you can believe in. With belief, comes success!

Unless....... You have no process....

Too many reps today, "wing it". Also, companies are throwing so many different ways to approach business and so many different tactics to get

to the sale that in large part, reps are confused and more often than not resort back to winging-it with marginal success.

My advice to you is, find the approach that best meets your personality. Step out of your comfort zone. Grow a little through success and failure and determine which process/strategy is best for you. Once you determine this, find a solution or product that you know can help.

With this process, comes the belief and ultimately the hope that will lead you to more wins and eventually more $$$$ and success.

Hope can be a sales strategy, but only if accompanied with belief and a process that is consistent and adjusted as needed. THAT is the most important thing!

And to paraphrase the VP of Selling Excellence at SAP, Shawn Robertson who once said at a Forrester Event, "The most important thing about the most important thing, is that the most important thing, REMAINS the most important thing". Words to live by as a sales rep. Don't you think?

Chapter 4

Frustrated? How to Re-define a Lead

and Limit COLD Calls!

One of the most difficult things to do for some sales people is to pick up the phone and make a cold call. Alternatively, a rep typically waits for an incoming lead or for marketing to create some magic and get their phone to ring. The general rule, depending on what type of business you are in is reps doing this type of selling are going to generally or eventually fail. Reps who are more often successful, supplement the incoming leads with a dedicated effort of outgoing action and calls.

The question is, how do you do this without feeling like the old guard. Who wants to feel like Willy Loman or a vacuum salesmen knocking on doors every evening?? Companies like *data.com* and *infoUSA* will make you believe that they have the answer, by giving you a large database of names and numbers to target and call upon. But at the end of the day, it is still a cold call, isn't it? You're still just knocking on a door....

Others like *Lattice Engines, InsideView and* D&B Hoovers, give you a reason to call based on some sort of news or event that is occurring there. Although this can be construed as a cold call, it really makes the life of the sales rep easier because it <u>helps them justify the outreach</u>. We all know how much a nuisance it is to receive those calls at 7:00 pm at night just as you are winding down, from the *National Order of Paper Deliverers* and the request for a donation! Think how hard it is for THAT person to make a call (.... but that's for another book all together!)

So how do you lessen the blow and redefine this interaction from a "nuisance" to "assistance"?

Looking deeper into the companies that offer this *warm up* capability, *RainKing, DiscoverOrg, InsideView, D&B Hoovers* and new comer *Artesian* generally stand alone because they look at all companies and utilize the web to pull these events.

The others isolate the companies you may be interested in only and then find news and events you may find interesting. But if you are not aware of a company, you won't be able to get the important information you need.

This is powerful information. Going back to the discussion of the cold call.... imagine now that you are a rep sitting and waiting for the incoming lead or marketing generated lead. But now, instead of just waiting, you were able to reach out to these new CTO's as outlined above and say, "I just read the PR announcing your appointment." <u>This call is now a little less cold isn't it?</u> This call may be a little bit more welcomed than the *smile and dial* tactics that some companies want their reps to engage in. A new CTO is not sitting on their hands doing nothing, rather they are looking or are going to be looking at EVERYTHING that makes their organization tick. From employees, to software, to technology, to you name it. This isn't looking so much like a cold call anymore.

Sometimes when I mention a trigger based approach, people respond by saying things like, "triggers won't work for me". That is a mind boggling statement. Let's think about that for a moment. Is it better to call a list of manufacturing companies and facilities people blindly because they meet your demographic and/or "sweet spot", cold? Or is it better to take that SAME list and find those that are expanding, hiring, winning contracts, building new facilities, experiencing a facilities management change, etc... etc... You name it. **If you are calling those companies *anyway*, why wouldn't you want to call the ones where you had a conversation starter teed up for you to open that door?? Why not top-size your targets?**

That's what a company like those mentioned can do for any company selling practically anything. Imagine a sales team leveraging this type of activity across multiple locations, selling multiple products and *ALSO* utilizing incoming marketing leads and opportunities.

No matter what you sell, a company experiencing a change is 10x's more likely to buy based on an event that is occurring at their location (http://shiftselling.com/trigger-event-selling/#.UzWKvKg7u-0).

The selling world is changing every day. From the original *Polk Directories*, to CD's, to post card mailing, to list sales, to email blasting to social selling techniques being utilized today. Companies need to evolve and change their way of thinking or be left behind. I truly believe that by investing in and committing to a trigger based selling approach, organizations will experience an immediate uptick in rep success. But it needs to be a consistent, daily re-enforced approach that each rep follows diligently.

Trigger based selling isn't a hobby.... it's an approach that more often than not, will open more doors and lead to more success!

Chapter 5

Where Is Your Next Sale Coming from?

The full disclosure here is; In the past, I have sold data and information and know the data industry quite well. Along with that I have also used many different providers through the years while leading different sales teams. So I have the unique perspective of speaking from both sides.

When working through a sales cycle and trying to profess the many great attributes and solutions that these different products offer (products like *D&B Hoovers, Rain King, DiscoverOrg, Data.com, Zoominfo* etc...), I am still taken aback by how many marketing and sales folks continue to chase the CONTACT and NOT the OPPORTUNITY.

You hear it quite consistently that *their* contact data is bad....
and *their* contact data is bad... and *THEIR* contact data is bad. So
we all need to come to a conclusion that .... contact data is
overall, *BAD!* I have heard from different gurus in the data
space that the average data accuracy is around 72% when
looking at the average, reputable database. To me, if that is the
case then 3 + out of every 10 calls will end up at the wrong or
missing person. I say, "BIG DEAL!"

Why do we continue as organizations to chase contacts?? Craig
Elias of SHiFT Selling (www.shiftselling.com) has a nice overview
that points out that 90% of the people we call are "status quo".
Basically, they are not buying anything. But everyday sales reps
continue to chase the contact and not the opportunity which
leads to minimal conversions.

Further, if we look at the many studies (and there are many....),
that outline the value of a **trigger based sales approach**, the
stats are overwhelmingly in favor of NOT chasing the contacts,
but rather focusing on companies that are undergoing a change

of some sort. Whether that change is a funding announcement, a fiscal year end, a new office opening or a management change.

Let's focus on the last 'trigger', a management change:

As mentioned in a previous chapter, **DiscoverOrg** did a study in Q3 of 2013 that stated, 80% of new managers taking over a new position spent money in the first 90-days of employment. WHAT?! 80%!!! Let's think about that.... If we could focus specifically on management changes, what would our odds be of securing a sale more so than doing the same old, same old of chasing contacts?

Further, **Forrester** did a study in 2012 (Buyer Insights), that stated 74% of all purchases occurred when a company was undergoing some sort of change. Once again, 74%!!

All the intelligence being received from the **Gartners,** the **Forresters,** the **Aberdeens,** et al, all point to finding the OPPORTUNITY to get to the sale. But every day, I speak to people that tell me the current data provider's contacts are not "up to snuff".

Ladies and Gentlemen, today I say to you.... STOP chasing CONTACTS and **focus on finding the OPPORTUNITIES** that will lead you to your next sale.

Focus on fiscal year end announcements where you KNOW budgets are freeing up. Focus on management changes where you KNOW, 80% of the time money will be spent in the first 90-days. Focus on new office openings and relocation announcements because you KNOW that they will be purchasing equipment, software, people, bandwith, advertising, etc... etc... etc...

To be a game changer, you need to change your game. Don't be fooled by database companies that wow you with BIG numbers of how many contacts and company records they have. But rather, focus on the companies that can deliver **large volumes** of event driven information that will put your next sale right into your lap. Think of it this way.... If you were in the recruiting space and called an HR person from a database that was no longer at the company you were trying to sell to, would you take your ball and go home? And if you did... are you really doing your best to open that door? Chances are that specific HR person is "status quo" anyways, but you would probably find another to speak to before finding there was no opportunity there and end up moving on. Conversely, if you focused on 20 companies that announced a hiring in a PR, or announced a new plant opening, or announced an expansion, or announced a funding announcement to add people, etc. and utilized a contact mentioned in the PR, or even better, used a contact granted from a database like _DiscoverOrg or RainKing_ for example, you now are chasing a real OPPORTUNITY. Not just the contact. You KNOW that they will make a human capital purchase based on all that is occurring. If your initial contact is wrong...SO WHAT! Find another. **They WILL buy** and if you can utilize the information you have found in your trigger, you will eventually find the right person to start your sales interaction.

It's easy enough to try this approach. The first time you try anything different is the most difficult. But making it a habit is focusing on this each and every day, finding triggers and attacking OPPORTUNITIES and not just CONTACTS!

Using a tool like these, will help you find the OPPORTUNITIES that make the most sense in your industry. Then have a solid process for following up. You may find you'll need to touch them 7, 8 or even 9 times before it resonates. But, be consistent. Be diligent. Be a sales rep.... And I bet you will see more doors will open for you than you have in the past.

Chapter 6

Are Your Prospects Pizza?

Driving into work one day, I had a thought as I watched cars zip in out of traffic on 495-N and watched others get close enough to the car in front of them at 75+ MPH that it coerced the person in the "lead" to pull aside and let them pass.

Imagine if we treated the lines at your last wedding buffet the same way. You riding Uncle Paul so tight that you can smell the back of his head until he is so uncomfortable he lets you ahead of him. Then you dart out and sprint 15 cousins ahead and slide in front of Aunt Josephine just in time for the "fresh" rigatoni.

Applying this same ridiculous analogy also applies to business and the prospecting that some sales and marketing organizations practice. Think about the last 20+years of ordering pizza. It's Saturday night; the gang is all there and someone says, let's get a pie. You reach for the phone book, flip to the "pizza" page where all the listings are. You pick one. Dial them up. And order your pie. Easy peazy!

As we in the sales game know, finding your next prospect isn't as easy as ordering pizza, but yet many organizations try the same tactics. Handing out business listings to find names and companies. **They push their teams to make 200 calls a day.** Smile and dial until they get a live one on the hook! But in this day and age does this make the most sense?

More and more studies show, that taking a more tactical approach to your prospecting will net you greater reward. As I continue to mention, DiscoverOrg **found that *80% of technology management changes would make a $1M+ dollar buying decision within their first 90-days on the job.*** Imagine if your team was focused on just these types of Management Changes. Could you see this as being more successful than the smile and dial approach?

Further, a study by ***Aberdeen Group*** in 2014, found that organizations that utilize a trigger based approach in their sales organizations had more reps attaining quota, had increased sales forecasting accuracy and had a higher retention rate among existing clients. In the same study they found that 79% of best in class organizations utilize triggers to make a first contact with a prospect.

If we think about it, it does make sense. Calling a new management change and congratulating them on a new appointment is an event that not nearly enough organizations take advantage of. New leaders are not sitting on their hands staying the course. They are looking at everything and anything to apply their ideas and make their mark quickly. Having discussions early in their tenure sets the buying vision and more often than not, puts you in the lead position in a potential purchase.

Apply the same type of logic to a company receiving venture capital to expand, a company hiring, a company opening a new office, a company launching a new CRM, opening a data center or launching a new product. There are countless events, or "triggers" that will put your sales organization in the right place at the right time and with a story to tell based on the event.

If you have never tried this approach, it's easy to get started. Tools like *RainKing, DiscoverOrg, InsideView, D&B Hoovers* and even Google Alerts, give your organization not only the triggers, but the volume of triggers needed to be successful. The global database will help your entire sales organization find the important events that are appropriate for the goods and services YOU sell. Along with the contacts and firmographic details all in one place.

Stop prospecting like you're ordering pizza! and create a streamline process of success.

Chapter 7

FREE BEER!

Email and Subject Lines

...Not really. Although it is a great way to grab someone's attention. I remember a *Warner Brothers* cartoon where the theater manager was trying to get people to come see his singing frog but couldn't get anyone to come until he posted his "Free Beer!" sign.

First off, let me preface this with, this is one man's opinion, but, selecting the right subject line in an email reach out campaign is just as important, if not even MORE important than the actual copy that accompanies it. If the recipient isn't intrigued by the subject line, then they won't open it and your content goes for naught.

The idea should be to make the subject line the least "salesy" line as   possible or else you are a commercial... and everyone HATES commercials.

Let's look at some of my recent SPAM and the subject lines used:

1. 6 strategies to quickly improve your sales skills

2. [Unnamed Company] just raised $50M - Here's how their marketing works

3. Solve your communication workflow problems

4. Explore Changes in Customer Service

5. What it takes to deliver the ultimate webinar

6. Can Setting Quotas Earlier Help Drive Better Results? You may be surprised...

Yuck! Yuck! Yuck! Yuck! Yuck! and Yuck!

These are all commercials. Who is opening these? Who is reading this? In my opinion.... nobody. The key to getting people to open your email (...and to avoid SPAM blockers) is to make the email look personal. Something as simple as; "Follow Up" or "Meeting" or "Hello Again" or "Your PR from This Morning"....

These won't work all the time either. There are so many *experts* who offer up subject lines as the greatest ones to use. Unfortunately, marketing is ALWAYS evolving which means HOT subject lines are also always evolving. Something that works today, may not work tomorrow... so don't get so stuck on a subject line that you get lazy and not try or create others as you continue to market each day.

These simple subject lines are not salesy at all. The objective is getting your recipient to open your email. If that goal is accomplished, then the next is to have pertinent information in your email that will allow you to have a conversation and ultimately **sell them with your spoken words rather than your written HTML.**

If you have a solution that you *KNOW* can help the masses, start laying off the long winded subject lines and simplify your outreach all together. You'll find more people are reading your emails and you will be having more conversations because of it.

Simplify! Give it a shot... you'll be surprised how well it works.

Chapter 8

What's Your "A" Player Definition?

.... a leader is what he wants the team to become."

In the next couple of chapters, I would like to focus on hiring and developing talent.

Everyone, at one point or another has heard the term or has been presented the question, "Are you an 'A' player?" or "How many 'A' players do you have on your team?" On the surface I think we all know what an 'A' player is. In this chapter, let's take a look at some of the traits that define this type of person...

I do believe the definition will vary depending on the type of manager you are... or if you are an individual contributor trying to convince yourself that you are indeed part of the "*A World*", but let me outline my definition and then I would love for you to take a mental inventory of what your 'A' player looks like:

1. **Personality** - I think in order to qualify; you need to be someone that others migrate to. Not just a loner that keeps to themselves and produces, but someone who is willing to help with an answer, jump in whenever needed and not look for anything more than the gratitude of helping another.

2. **Work Ethic** - This is a little tough to gauge only because I think sometimes we get lost in quota achievement, which is the top priority in a sales role, but I have seen many talented people content with just hitting or getting close to their number when I know they could be killing it. I have had many marginal A's (which are not bad to have by the way), that get close to their number every month or every quarter, but are more the 8:30 am to 5:30 type. If they could spend a little more time on the job could they achieve more? This is not to say an A player can't be a 9 to 5'er, because some do spend every minute of their day trying to be as successful as possible. But I do think this drive to always achieve more makes a person an A.

3. **Desire to Learn** - The old saying that when we stop learning we stop growing holds true in so many walks of life. I think

sometimes human beings get content in what they know and fail to keep learning. Learning keeps things fresh. The more you apply yourself to know everything you possibly can about your business and the products you sell, your industry and your competition, will ultimately make you better and be a part of the A player definition. Knowledge breeds confidence, which we all need in any interaction.

4. **Achievement** - Let's face it, without this part nobody can truly be perceived as an A player, can they? The people I would consider A's that have worked with me in the past are never content with being marginal. They have a steely-eyed desire to achieve assigned targets and surpass them. These people when short of a goal or a number will do everything in their power to find more pipeline, ask for help, learn more and look for other ways to ensure their success whether it be now or tomorrow or next week or next month (.... ties back to work ethic in many ways).

5. **Self-starter** - This is another tough to define trait, but I think it also ties in with some of the other traits we have discussed.

There is a fine line from sitting and suffering in silence over asking a question to get the answer so you can move on. I think the most successful reps want to be able to be independent and only escalate things when they absolutely have to. Also, I think having a manager that will teach you to fish instead of catching you a fish is a must. This goes along with their *desire to learn* and once they see how it can be done, utilizing the knowledge to advance themselves in their role.

In summary, these are the traits I think make up my A player. At the end of the day too though, we as a manager or a supervisor, also need to be A players. Not fall into the *do as I say and not as I do mentality,* but rather be a leader, be supportive and perhaps coerce the A out of a fringe player.

John Wooden once said,

> **"…. a leader is what he wants the team to become."**

Truer words have not been spoken. It's on us as leaders as much as it is on those that work for us to lead in a way to maximizes the talent on our teams.

Chapter 9

Success and Hiring to "Pay it Forward"

Managing teams over the years, I have learned that no matter how hard you work, it seldom translates into success unless the important people...those that report to you, have the same desire for success. And understanding what "success" is, should determine how you hire and how you promote, just as much as sales success.

I have hired many sales people over the years and many of them have one on to be successful and others may have not experienced the same level of success, but my hope is that each of them have learned something that will make them better in their next endeavor, whether it be at my company or if they move on.

When looking to hire a new sales rep, we all look to the numbers and the resume to understand what they have done in the past, where they have come from, what they have earned and how it may translate into a new role with your company. Although these are important, I also like to understand what the potential of the person I am hiring is and can I give them a chance to be successful. Simply, do they have the drive and desire to "pay it forward"....

I remember two individuals specifically that did not have the resume or credentials that would separate them from some of the others I had spoken to. On paper, they were just a step behind. But during the interview process, I liked their drive, I liked their desire, I liked their perspective on life and what they could do if given the chance to join my sales team. Giving someone who is relatively new to the work force a chance at success is the same chance that was given to me years ago and I still am very appreciative of that opportunity.

The two individuals I mention have both gone on to lead their own teams and make their own contributions to the "pay it forward", mentality. They experienced great success with me and outgrew their roles and quickly moved on to more important, higher earning roles. But if not given the opportunity, where would they be today? How many of us have similar stories?

Success is not measured by the amount you acquire through the years, rather success should be measured by the amount of lives you can affect positively in the leadership role you possess....

....and of course, hitting your sales numbers helps too!

Chapter 10

"NO" is the Second Best Answer a Prospect Can

Give a Sales Rep!

In this chapter I will try not to sound like a public service announcement, so be warned....

Sitting in on many forecast meetings over the years, I have spoken to and seen sales reps who will show up with the same companies in their forecast week after week after week after week. In many instances a sales manager's first instinct is to blame it on the rep for not being able to forecast correctly, or not working hard enough to ask the right questions to move a deal ahead. In many instances, this can be true, but still in others it's the inability to get a hold of your decision maker.

.... I love the example of that particular *Seinfeld* episode where Kramer decided he would turn the tables on the cable company. Instead of the cable guy not showing up for his assigned appointment time again, Kramer instead would make an appointment and then not be there when the cable guy showed up at his apartment. The cable guy would keep making appointments and Kramer would keep missing them until they finally met up and discussed the pain and suffering that was being inflicted and THEN all was finally good between them. Let's focus on that...."pain and suffering". Now of course I say that facetiously, but when a decision maker goes silent for long stretches of time, there is definitely **mental anguish** that is felt by the sales rep. Both by not knowing if they will secure the sale, but also applied by their sales management team continuously asking about the particular deal that seems to be showing up each week in their forecast.

So the question is... Why do so many decision makers go silent? I have always made it a point to let a potential vendor know where they stand and where they are in the sales process mainly because of the experiences I, as well as my reps have experienced. Whether that is a car salesman, magazine sales guy, insurance sales guy, a real estate agent or a marketing automation/SaaS/CRM or whatever sales rep.

As leaders in organizations, shouldn't we all act the same? In essence, **treat a sales rep as we wish our sales reps to be treated.**

Too often a rep goes the extra mile to demonstrate a service, prepare documentation, complete follow ups, fight for pricing, travel and much more to work towards the 'YES" they eventually desire. Many times the interest is there, budget is set aside and all is progressing well enough for a rep to feel confident enough to forecast based on the fact that they know:

- They have the decision maker

- They have isolated budget

- There is a need

- They can solve the issue/problem

- They have buy-in from all parts of the organization

More so, at times even agreements have gone through legal red-lines or NDA's are in place and more.... But still there is silence. In many instances, sometimes weeks will go by where there is no contact. Emails, voice mails, *Linked-In* in-mails, texts all can be used to make a connection all for a simple answer to the question, "...are we still progressing"? With every means of outreach, frustration grows.

Decision makers are busy. That is a given. And sometimes their priorities are elsewhere, which is understandable. But we all need to make a better effort to let sales reps know where they stand. No sales rep enjoys pestering a prospect. Who would? But sometimes there is no alternative. If everyone and everything is pointing you back to the same person and that person is not giving you an answer, it becomes a very frustrating sales process and in many instances relationships can be damaged. Not a good way to start with a new potential customer or vice versa.

Think of how much email and VM's we all could avoid by just saying, "NO" early in the sales process when we know that a solution won't work for us. We are potentially disappointing a rep that we may have developed a relationship with, but in the end they can go focus their attention where they can eventually get the "YES" they need and everyone is better for it. Like Kramer and his cable guy.

Let's all commit today! We will start treating the vendors we are dealing with the same way we want our reps to be treated. Easy enough task. So next time you're in a sales interaction, think about how your simple yes or no can benefit both you and the sales person who is trying to win your business. So shall it be written, so shall it be done!

Chapter 11

Transition

*"In order to succeed in life, your fear of failure cannot exceed
your desire for success"*

Transition.... A simple word, but sometimes very difficult to act on. In the business world (....and even in the personal world), too many of us remain comfortable even in situations where you know there could be greener pastures. Being comfortable and not wanting to engage in a *transition* of sorts could leave you in the same "dead-end" job or relationship for far too long. So why is it so hard to realize that a change is necessary?

Human nature directs all of us to be creatures of habit. For example; You drive to work the same way every day. Tuesday night is always taco night. You sit in the same spot at the weekly meeting you attend and have attended for years. We force ourselves into a rut and many times it's hard to work ourselves out of it. When we stop learning and challenging ourselves, we stop growing intellectually and as a person. If we never step out of that comfort zone, we will never realize what we could possibly and potentially accomplish by taking on the *transition* into something new.

But sometimes with *transition*, comes fear. I once heard a quote that went something like this:

"In order to succeed in life, your fear of failure cannot exceed your desire for success"

This holds true in so many walks of life. Whether it's sports, a relationship or especially your professional career. This applies to me personally. Many years ago, I was working at 3M Company in Rochester, NY. I was making what I thought was decent money for a twenty-something year old, but I wasn't challenged. After almost 6 years in this "rut", my elder brother, Frank sat me down and we had a life-changing discussion. He said to me, if you're not happy... make a change. But how I wondered? I have a car payment. I have a mortgage. I have commitments. His refrain to me was simple... you choose to have a car and a house, so you choose to remain comfortable, even though you may not be happy. You don't *have* to have those things. You *choose* to.

He was right. At the time, I had no children and was not married. If ever there was a time to make a change, it was now.

So I took his advice (...he later said I was CRAZY and he didn't mean it literally - but it was the best advice I ever received!). That Monday, I quit my job and booked a flight to Florida. I always wanted to live there and now I had the time and some money to at least chase this desire. It would be a difficult *transition*, but I needed to take the chance.

To make a long story a bit shorter (too late???), on that trip I met my eventual wife of 19+ years and together we have raised three wonderful children. I eventually secured a job with PageNet, where I met a GM that would transfer me to Boston and helped set me on my way to where I am living and what I am doing today. All because of a conversation with my brother, Frank. If I never took the chance, where would I be today? I often wonder....

Not all stories will end like mine, but more of us need to take the chance at something new and find the happiness you deserve. Challenge yourself. Every day! Ask yourself this question; Is it better to try and do the things you think you can accomplish, rather than to sit idle and regret later in life that you never gave it a fair shake?

Getting started is easy and **doesn't** *necessarily mean* **quitting your job**. If you are in a rut and feeling unhappy, try breaking the rut. Do something different. Drive to work via an alternate route. Have pot roast instead of tacos on Tuesday. Force yourself to sit in a different seat at that next meeting. Challenge yourself. Take on a new project at work. Volunteer to lead a group or a task. Challenging yourself and doing it different is in sorts a *transition* from the norm. This may be all you need to break free and find a sense of purpose and accomplishment, and in some sense happiness.

Chapter 12

Got Your Rolodex Ready?

As a leader of a sales organization, one of the hardest things to do is to get a new rep up to speed and selling quickly. Whether you're selling small ticket items or even enterprise solutions; all new incoming sales reps will need to hit the ground running to impact your sales numbers as fast, and with as little pain as possible.

Being that it's 2018 and we are in an age of information that is more advanced than ever before, I still get a kick out of job postings that say, ".... must have a Rolodex of potential prospects". Really? The fact that, the term "Rolodex" is still being used in a posting would make me look elsewhere if I was in the market and trying to secure a job. How forward thinking is this company and how vested are they in providing me the tools to help make me successful?

The stats say that 90% of the world's data has been created in the last 2 years. WHAT? That's crazy to comprehend. 90%! There is so much information out there that companies are drowning in a sea of data which places them in a position of asking incoming reps to bring a "Rolodex" with them. Further, with so much competition out there for premium talent, more so than ever before a sales rep can choose their next position and much like LeBron James, "Take their talents...." to wherever they want.

So how can companies and Sales Leaders first, attract top talent and then secondly provide them the opportunity for success? Well, one way is to provide them a database. Not an old, stale legacy database from a company CRM that has been handed down to rep after rep, who one after the other has failed. But a database of fresh companies and contacts.

First let's think about how hard it is to attract top talent. In a race to secure the "A" players consider telling a prospective new sales rep that you will give them access to a database of not only companies and contacts to call, but the ability to segment territories, cut through demographics, educate on SWOT reports and corporate family structure as well as isolate existing and new companies that are more likely to need the services that they will be potentially selling. Marketing will always deliver a set of leads to your sales teams, but letting a rep know that you will give them the tools to be successful in the interview process will set you apart from those that are asking for a Rolodex.

So now imagine this same reps first day. You get them trained and ready to go and out of the gate, they have people to call. Why? Because you have isolated companies that have secured venture capital, or companies building new facilities, or new RFP's or new leaders in companies being appointed. If the rep is calling and securing appointments at ground zero, then how much quicker will they be adding revenue in your pipeline and eventually closing business?

Some enterprise reps take up to TWELVE months to build a pipeline and have an impact on YOUR number. SMB reps can take anywhere from three to six months to make any type of impact. So why are we as sales leaders not giving them what they need out of the gate to shorten these cycles and realize the benefit that much quicker?

Services, like the many that have been mentioned up to this point can be used to help you "close" that "A" player and get them on your team. Once on your team, they will have the resources they need to build a territory and a list of targets that in the past, were not so easy to come by. Many services act as a big phone book of names and numbers for your new reps to call upon with no "*signal*" of a buying opportunity. Find a service that will tap into many contacts and many companies and more importantly, many trigger events globally and isolate the *Business Signals* that WILL alert your new rep to companies more likely to buy based on events occurring at their location. The more interactions like this early on in their tenure, means more pipeline and a quicker ramp to a fully effective head for you!

Imagine trying to isolate a CTO at a "green" company that does business in China that has recently been awarded a government contract? How would you get that information today? Google? Trade Journal? Somewhere else? D&B Hoovers, for example will pull this information together in seconds and even better have the contacts and the corresponding information in the reps view in seconds of their initial search.

As the leaders of your respective sales organizations, how can you afford NOT to provide your team with all the tools they need to be successful? Relying on Marketing and the Rolodex will only get you part of the way there. Try pitching the idea of a database like *D&B Hoovers* in your next interview. You will attract more top talent than you ever have before.

Chapter 13

Is there Magic in Those TRIGGERS?

After all these years of managing sales teams and spending the majority of them professing the gold that is found in calling on triggers, I wanted to put my money where my mouth is.

In 2015, as an organization, we closed roughly $200k in sales the previous year, specifically utilizing the triggers found in our own solution. I noticed however that although the processes were in place, the triggers were not being worked in a manner that could maximize the success of calling on them. Reps would find a trigger, mostly new VP's of sales or marketing and send them a congratulatory email and maybe follow up with a call. Sometimes the new hire would respond and when they did the deals closed faster and most of the time for more revenue than our average.

But what if we worked them more consistently?

Just like in *Glengarry Glen Ross* there was growing sentiment among my team that the incoming marketing driven leads were, "weak". My retort to the team was work the triggers at the same time and work them consistently. Then it hit me. What if I took all the triggers for a period and worked them myself? Sort of a hiatus from Directing the team. Instead I would roll up my sleeves and be my own company's case study.

I started in October of that year using a VP of Sales and Marketing, CMO and other marketing related functions trigger alert. Each time a new appointment was received, I would be alerted and I would send an email saying congrats and follow up with a voicemail on the same day. I set up a process where if after a day I didn't hear from them, on day three I would send a follow up email or voicemail. I would mix it up each time. If I still hadn't received a response by day five, I would send a meeting request via email. Each time I referenced their new appointment and their need to review all processes in their early days and how I could help.

If still no response came, I would have a day 7 email ready with a subject line of "One More Try". In this email I would apologize for the multiple attempts to connect, but still ask for 10 minutes to discuss our services. I would also follow this email with a voicemail. All emails were set up as templates in our CRM, salesforce.com. The process was easy and consistent. I was pulling 5 sometimes 10 a day.

By the end of week one I was averaging 2 to 3 responses a day. All on my own. No leads from marketing. I was doing demos every day and immediately building a pipeline. By week three I had closed my first deal, a new VP of Marketing at a gas cylinder supplier. In that same week I started having more advanced conversations with an EVP of Marketing from a big data analytics consultant. Then another with an SVP of a software company who sold specifically to brokerage firms and wealth management companies. Heck this was easy. I thought, "there

IS magic in these triggers". But the magic needs to be followed with a process. Consistent follow up, leads to more conversations, which leads to more demos, which leads to more pipeline.

By the time I reached week 8. I had closed several deals all because of a first intro from a trigger. The deals were closing quicker than the teams average AND for more revenue. My pipeline was solid and I had enough in a more advanced stage that I would more than exceed a quota of a sales rep on our sales team. All from triggers? All from the "magic"? Well, sort of. The magic of triggers along with the process that leads to success. That's the ultimate magic.

I am my own case study. I am proof that what the Aberdeen's and Gartner's and the Forrester's of the world are saying is true. A trigger event IS more likely to lead to a sale. This stuff, as I have been saying for many years actually works. And it works even better than expected if you work the process and even more importantly, work it consistently.

Chapter 14

Competition. Competition. Competition

How Do You Choose the Right Vendor

So now that you have a process and potentially some new ways to go after your market, who are you going to use to get you there?

In this chapter we will look closer at how to choose your perfect vendor.

Have you ever asked yourself why does *McDonald's* open a new store right across the street from *Burger King*? Why does *Starbucks* think it's a good idea to put their new store right next to *Dunkin Donuts*? How many *NAPA Auto Parts* have you seen within a hop, skip and jump from an *AutoZone*? The answer to all these is because competition is good. None of the competitors are really that much better or worse than the others. It's all a matter of taste or perspective.

We have spoken at length of the many offerings in the previous chapters. But when looking at the vast offerings of data solution products out in the marketplace, there are so many it will make your head spin. Data cleansing, data enrichment, data organization, data, data, data. Some use partnerships and help create the "golden record", others utilize web-crawling, still others use artificial intelligence and some companies use components of all of them. I truly believe **each** has the ability to help your organization and none of them launch their products or go into business thinking their solution is worse than their competition or that they will be unsuccessful in selling it. You can be successful using **ANY** of them as long as you are <u>committed</u> to the success of your purchase.

So how do you best choose the vendor that will work for your organization? Well, I see a few factors that go into this:

1. **Budget**: How much are you willing to spend? Many of the less expensive solutions will get you 95% of what the more expensive products deliver. You need to weigh the benefits

of the "nice to haves", over the "gotta haves" and that remaining 5%. Much like when buying a car or a house or a number of high-ticket items, you buy what you can afford (or at least you should). Are you strictly looking for companies and contacts that you can segment for your teams to call? If so, do you need analyst reports? Do you need SWOT reports? Do you need corporate family? Or are these just nice to haves that you will seldom utilize? These will add to the cost of your solution and may make it harder for you to realize a return on the purchase. Know what you need and don't be sold additional bells and whistles that you will need to pay for that your team most likely will not use.

2. **Integration**: It's amazing to me how many companies don't use CRM. If you are not leveraging a CRM today for you or your sales team, stop reading this now and start researching to purchase one immediately. There are many, and some are free depending on the size of your organization. *HubSpot, SugarCRM, Salesforce, Zoho, MS Dynamics* and even *ACT!* are all potential CRM's that you should be using. And when you choose a CRM, understand the data solutions that integrate,

seamlessly with the CRM. If you are tasked with purchasing the tools for your organization, the hardest thing for you will be internal user adoption after you make your purchase. The easiest way to get user adoption is to have the tools you want the team to use, to speak to each other and become a part of their daily routine. If a rep is logging into a CRM every day to get the company and contact info they need to make their calls or email outreach, why not have the data they need to be successful directly tied within the CRM? This will keep them in one platform to minimize the distractions. Be sure there is some integration between your data and the CRM and you will see that user adoption will be almost unanimous across the board, which in the end, makes you look good.

3. **Predictive Events**: If you have made it this far into this book, then by now you know how I feel about predictive events or triggers and their value on a sales organization's outreach. You give me a sales team and a tool that brings forth management changes, new office openings, funding announcements and other event announcements... and I will

outsell your sales team that is just cold calling using a company database tool all day long. Organizations experiencing change are buying period! Whether that is hiring people, buying new equipment, software, furniture, you name it. If they are experiencing a trigger they will buy and if you can get there before the competition, you will win! When researching for a data provider, be sure they can get you these types of alerts but also be sure you are prepared to school your teams on the importance of these and establish a well thought out process on how to attack these.

"You give me a sales team and a tool that brings forth management changes, new office openings, funding

announcements and other event announcements...

and I will outsell your sales team that is just cold calling using

a company database tool all day long"

4. **Web-Crawling**: One of the more frustrating things a sales person will experiences is when a tool you are given by your company has outdated information. This is almost

unavoidable due to the constant flux that organizations are under as people leave for greener pastures or restructuring occurs and the data providers have trouble keeping up. And if you just rolled out your data solution as the greatest thing since sliced bread, it won't take long for your sales reps to lose confidence in the solution because of errors and stop using it all together creating another "shelf ware" for you. Some of this can be avoided if the provider delivers triggers as mentioned above. If the trigger exists, it is a real lead, and now it's up to your sales rep to find the appropriate person (...which more than likely is in the article of the trigger anyway). Companies that utilize a daily, weekly or even monthly crawler are more likely to have accurate data. These crawlers visit websites and read things like the 'team management' page, 'about us' page, 'contact us' page and more. Who better to keep accurate data on a company than the companies themselves? Understanding who is utilizing web-crawling and how much of their data comes from this is key to a successful relationship with your data provider.

5. **Training/Help**: Again, I am always surprised at how many organizations don't utilize training that is offered up by vendors. As user friendly as some tools look to be, there are always subtle nuances that you and your team will be unaware of that may help you uncover the deal you need to get the ROI that will substantiate your purchase. If the data provider you are purchasing from doesn't have a training program or at minimum help video's, I don't feel that they are vested in your success. Conversely, if they do and you are not utilizing it, then you may be the one not vested in the success. Choose a vendor that WANTS you to be successful and can sell you on how they will make your team successful not just during the sale process, but even AFTER the sale is completed.

6. **Trial Period**: Be sure that you just don't take your vendors word for it. If they are not offering a trial of their solution, they may be this centuries version of a snake oil sales man.

Being confident in your product, means you are willing to let someone "bang around" in it for a while to prove that it will do the things you need it to do to be successful. And if you are given a trial, be sure you utilize it properly. No vendor enjoys a disgruntled customer AFTER a purchase and AFTER a 2-week trial period. If you are given a trial, this is your time to say this product is or isn't for me. A trial is what you will use to confidently choose the proper vendor for you.

7. **Commitment and Process**: Commit to your choice when it's all said and done. If your average sales price is $25,000 and you just paid $25,000 for your data provider, commit to finding one or two deals that will help you break even or even better, more than pay for it. Have a tracking mechanism in place to track leads or opportunities that come from your data choice (...Another reason to have CRM integration by the way). Stay close to your team's login activity... see if triggers are being utilized... pass out events to the team and show them how to act on them. Some light to heavy lifting up front, will make you a superstar later and justify your choice of vendors.

Wrapping it Up...

No matter who you select, if you do the proper due diligence upfront and commit yourself and your team to the success of the solution, you really can't make a bad decision. Set the expectation up front that utilizing the CRM integrated aspects of the product along with a predictive event approach benefits them and how it will benefit them. Let them know that you are aware that they will come across bad data from time to time. That's natural, but give your team the additional resources they need to quickly transition and create a successful Data/CRM/Sales Engagement strategy that will work for your whole sales organization.

Conclusion

Bringing it Home

Hopefully you have gleamed some useful information in the preceding chapters. Calling a company with a reason is the NUMBER ONE thing you can start doing today and begin to be more successful. Adding a consistent process to this engagement strategy will exponentially help you on your journey to success.

Whether you are a sales person or a sales manager, with any approach, process and consistency is what will lead you to your goals. Don't do anything half-way. Commit to it and decide if the new process is something that can work for you.

Remember, you are not defined by your past mistakes in sales. They have prepared you for your future success. Every interaction you ever had was a learning experience to make you better. Take the failures as direction on how to improve. Don't wallow in them. Use them to your advantage. And likewise, use the wins to further hone your skills and do your best to replicate them.

It has worked for me, and I am hoping you too can experience some of the success that I have been lucky enough to achieve!

I wish you and your teams much success and hope that I have helped you think about how to better yourself with a little "ketchup" for your Cheeseburger....

Bon appétit and Happy Selling !

Ketchup for Your Sales Process

Cover Design: Roger Ciliberto

Cover Design: Roger Ciliberto

3LConsulting Group
ISBN-13: 978-0578208039
ISBN-10: 0578208032
BISAC: Business & Economics / Skills

Roger Ciliberto
3LConsulting Group
Hilton NY 14468 – 781-330-8480

Printed in the United States of America

www.ingramcontent.com/pod-product-compliance
Lightning Source LLC
Chambersburg PA
CBHW050522210326
41520CB00012B/2409